40x 10/14 4/15

22x 12
7/10
1/12
4/13

D0819797

Sharks

by Lucia Raatma

Content Advisers: Terrence E. Young Jr., M.Ed., M.L.S.,
Jefferson Parish (La.) Public Schools, and Janann Jenner, Ph.D.

Reading Adviser: Dr. Linda D. Labbo,
Department of Reading Education, College of Education,
The University of Georgia

COMPASS POINT BOOKS

Minneapolis, Minnesota

Compass Point Books
3722 West 50th Street, #115
Minneapolis, MN 55410

Visit Compass Point Books on the Internet at *www.compasspointbooks.com* or e-mail your request
to *custserv@compasspointbooks.com*

Photographs ©: International/Jeff Rotman, cover; Roger Klocek/Visuals Unlimited, 4; Randy
Morse/Tom Stack & Associates, 5, 11; Ken Lucas/Visuals Unlimited, 6; Doug Perrine/Jose
Castro/Innerspace Visions, 7 (top); Jeff Rotman, 7 (bottom), 9, 12, 14, 15, 20–21, 26, 30, 34, 37, 41,
42; Mark A. Stack/Tom Stack & Associates, 8; Ed Robinson/Tom Stack & Associates, 10; Svetlana
Zhurkina, 13; Hal Beral/Visuals Unlimited, 16; Richard Ellis/Innerspace Visions, 19; Michael S.
Nolan/Tom Stack & Associates, 22–23; David B. Fleetham/Visuals Unlimited, 24, 31; Tom
Stack/Tom Stack & Associates, 25; A. Kerstitch/Visuals Unlimited, 27; Ferrari/Watt/Innerspace
Visions, 28; Rick Martin, 29; Universal/Archive Photos, 32; Unicorn Stock Photos/Mary Morina/A.
Gurmankin, 33; Mark Strickland/Innerspace Visions, 35; Marc Epstein/Visuals Unlimited, 36;
David B. Fleetham/Seapics.com/Innerspace Visions, 38; Jack Reid/Tom Stack & Associates, 40;
Jeff Greenberg/Visuals Unlimited, 43; XNR Productions, Inc., 46.

Editors: E. Russell Primm and Emily J. Dolbear
Photo Researcher: Svetlana Zhurkina
Photo Selector: Linda S. Koutris
Designer: Bradfordesign, Inc.

Library of Congress Cataloging-in-Publication Data
Raatma, Lucia.
  Sharks / by Lucia Raatma.
    p. cm. — (First reports)
    ISBN 0-7565-0056-7 (lib. bdg.)
    1. Sharks—Juvenile literature. [1. Sharks. 2. Endangered species.] I. Title. II. Series.
QL638.9 .R23 2001
597.3—dc21   00-010913

Table of Contents

The Amazing Shark

▲ *The jaws of a giant extinct shark*

People love to tell stories about sharks. Some stories are old sea tales. Some stories are scary. These stories are fun but they tell only a small part of what we now know about sharks.

Sharks are amazing animals. They have lived on Earth for millions of years. They live in waters all over the world.

▲ *The horn shark lives in the Pacific Ocean.*

▲ *The epaulette shark is spotted.*

There are about 370 different kinds of sharks. Most sharks are strong. Many swim very fast.

Sharks can be many different colors. Some are off-white or brown. Others are blue. Some sharks are gray or black. Some sharks are even spotted or

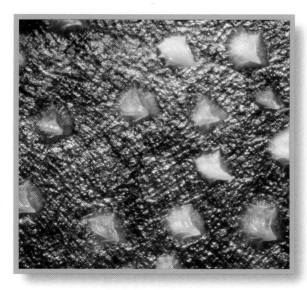

▲ *A close-up view of sharkskin*

striped. A shark's skin looks smooth. But if you touch it, it feels as sharp as teeth.

Most sharks have long, rounded bodies. A few sharks are smaller and fatter. The angel shark is almost flat.

▲ *A shark's shape helps it move through the water with ease.*

A shark's bones are not hard and solid. They are made of a soft tissue called **cartilage**. Shark cartilage allows the animals to move and turn easily. Humans have cartilage in their ears and nose and at the end of some bones.

Most sharks have long, pointed heads. They also have several rows of teeth. Their teeth are shaped like triangles and are very sharp. Sharks keep losing teeth throughout their lives. They grow new teeth to replace the old ones.

▲ *When a shark loses a tooth, it grows a new one.*

How Do Sharks Breathe?

▲ *The gills of a tiger shark*

Sharks breathe through openings in their bodies. These openings are called **gills**. Sharks have several pairs of gills. They take in **oxygen** when water passes over their gills.

Most sharks have to swim in order to breathe. They have to keep water moving past their gills.

How Do Sharks Swim?

Sharks swim through water by moving their bodies and tails from side to side. They steer with their fins. A fin works like your arm does when you're swimming.

Some fins are on the shark's back. Some are underneath the shark's body. A shark's tail also has fins.

▲ *The white-tip shark has several fins.*

▲ *A blue shark moves quickly through the water.*

Some sharks swim very fast. Many can swim three or four times faster than people. A blue shark can swim almost 40 miles (64 kilometers) per hour. Their quickness in the water can make them seem very frightening to people.

How Do Sharks See, Hear, and Smell?

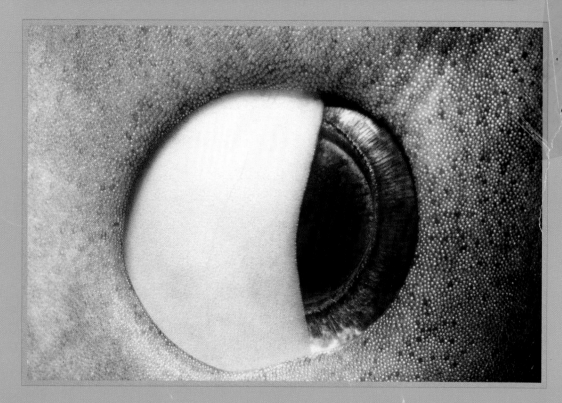

▲ The eye of a tiger shark

Sharks do not see the same way that people do. They see well in very dim light. Light reflects inside the shark's eyes. With this light, they can tell that objects are nearby. They do not see color or details as well as people do.

Sharks do not hear the way people do either. They have no ears. Instead, they have thin **canals** of water that run along the sides of their bodies. These canals are like tubes under the animal's skin. They are attached to nerves that send messages to the shark's brain. In this way, sharks can feel the sound waves around them. They can hear very low-pitched sounds.

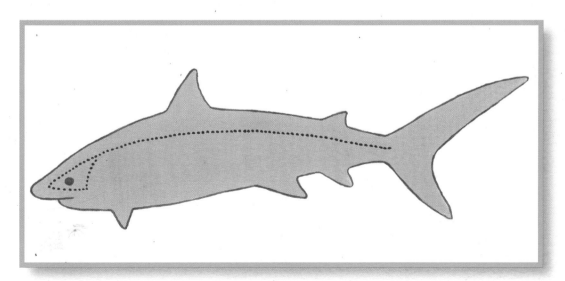

▲ *The canals that run under a shark's skin help it hear.*

▲ *This shark can smell the tuna bait that has been dropped into the water.*

The sense of smell is a shark's most important sense. Sharks are **predators**. A predator is a creature that hunts and kills other animals for food. Sharks can smell the animals they are hunting. In fact, their sense of smell is strongest when they are hungry.

What Do Sharks Eat?

Sharks eat many of the animals found in the water around them. They eat tiny plants and animals that float in the water. These plants and animals are called **plankton**. Sharks also eat crabs, sea turtles, seals, porpoises, clams, and fish.

▲ *A basking shark feeding on plankton*

Sharks can live for a long time without eating. Their bodies store fat. Sharks can live off their stored fat for months.

When sharks eat, they do not chew. They swallow their food whole. If a piece of food is too large to swallow, the shark rips it into smaller pieces before eating it.

▲ *Sharks often swallow their food whole.*

Where Do Sharks Live?

Sharks are found all over the world. Most live in warm water. Some live in cold water. For example, Greenland sharks live in the Arctic Ocean.

Most sharks live in saltwater. But some types of sharks live in freshwater.

▲ *The Greenland shark lives in icy northern ocean waters.*

Baby Sharks

▲ *A swell shark is born from an egg.*

Baby sharks are called **pups**. Some sharks lay eggs that hatch into pups. Some sharks give birth to live pups. Several pups born at the same time to the same mother are called a **litter**. There may be from two to twenty pups in a litter.

▲ *A lemon shark is born live.*

Types of Sharks

Many kinds of sharks are harmless to people. Other kinds of sharks can be very dangerous.

The great white shark is a fierce predator. It can swallow creatures up to half its size— seals, dolphins, and even other sharks. This shark has also attacked boats and swimmers.

The great white shark is the second largest of all the sharks. It is faster and stronger than most other sharks.

A great white shark swims by a researcher ▷
in a protective cage.

The largest shark is the whale shark. It eats only small fish and plankton. It is harmless to people.

Whale sharks weigh up to 20 tons. These giant sharks can grow to be 60 feet (18 meters) long. They are called whale sharks because they are as large as whales. They also eat the same kinds of food.

Whale sharks move slowly in the water. They swim by moving their whole bodies from side to side.

Whale sharks swim so slowly that ships sometimes bump into them.

A whale shark with a snorkeler ▶

The tiger sand shark is a dangerous shark. It lives in the warm oceans of the world and eats just about anything. It eats fish, seabirds, turtles, and even garbage thrown from ships. Some tiger sand sharks have eaten tin cans and clothing.

▲ *A tiger sand shark*

The bull shark is dangerous to people too. This shark is also called a ground shark. It sometimes swims inland up rivers.

▲ *A bull shark*

▲ *A hammerhead shark*

The hammerhead shark is well named. Its head looks like a hammer. Its flat face is shaped like the letter T. Its eyes and nostrils are at the ends of the "hammer."

Mako sharks are fast swimmers and great jumpers. They can swim more than 50 miles (80 kilometers) per hour. They can leap higher than 20 feet (6 meters).

Mako sharks are blue and white. They have long, pointed faces. They are also called blue pointers.

▲ *A mako shark*

Thresher sharks are strong swimmers too. These sharks flap their tails to strike their **prey**. They also flap their long tails to frighten fish into a group. Then the shark can catch a lot of fish at one time.

▲ *A thresher shark*

The smallest shark is the dwarf lantern shark. It measures only about 5 inches (13 centimeters) long.

Dwarf lantern sharks live in the deepest, darkest part of the ocean. That's why scientists only recently discovered them. Because it is so dark where they live, it is impossible to photograph a live dwarf lantern shark.

▲ *A drawing of a dwarf lantern shark*

How Do Sharks Act?

Most sharks prefer to swim alone. They are not usually found in groups, or **schools**, like other fish.

Sometimes three or more sharks have a **feeding frenzy**. Sharks in a feeding frenzy attack and eat anything and everything around them. A feeding frenzy usually starts when sharks smell blood.

▲ *Sharks in a feeding frenzy*

▲ *The jaws of a great white shark*

When a shark attacks, it moves quickly. It raises its nose and pushes forward with its upper jaw. Then, the shark closes its mouth and sinks its teeth into its prey.

Some people think sharks are dangerous to people. But only a few types of sharks have ever attacked humans. In fact, many types of sharks are completely harmless. The sharks most likely to attack people are the great white shark and the bull shark.

▲ *Sharks, like the one in this ad for the movie* Jaws, *sometimes mistake people for other animals.*

Sometimes sharks attack people because they mistake people for another kind of animal. For example, a shark may see a person's legs hanging over a surfboard. To the shark, a person on a surfboard may look like a sea lion or large fish.

▲ *The movie* Jaws *scared millions of viewers around the world.*

Some movies and books have given sharks a bad name. Many people fear sharks so much that they are afraid to swim in the ocean. However, there are not as many shark attacks on humans as some people think.

Sharks in Trouble

▲ *Sharks are often misunderstood by people.*

Some people think sharks are so dangerous that they should all be killed. If they knew more about these animals, however, they would see that there is little to fear.

Some sharks are killed when they are caught in fishing nets. Fishers put large nets in the water to catch fish. Sometimes sharks swim into the nets. These sharks often drown or die of hunger. Other sea animals, such as dolphins, also swim into nets by mistake.

▲ *Fishing nets are dangerous to sharks.*

▲ Some people fish for sharks.

People are a shark's greatest enemy. Some people kill sharks for sport. Some people hunt sharks to sell the animal's fins, teeth, and other body parts.

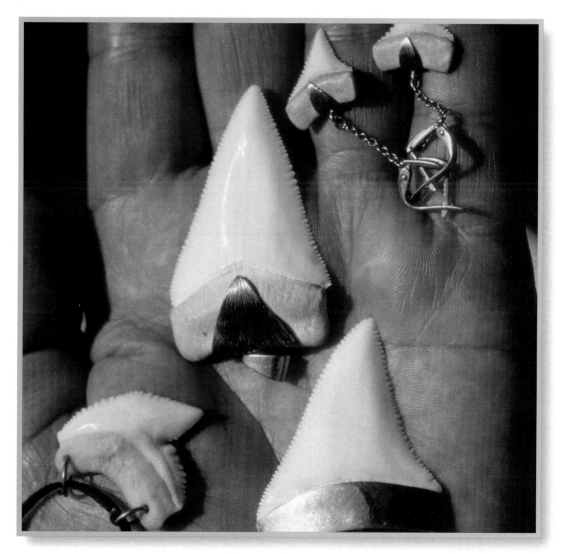

▲ *Various parts of a shark's body are valued by buyers.*

Why Are Sharks Important?

The number of sharks in the world is getting smaller. If there were no more sharks in our waters, the earth would soon be in trouble. Sharks are important to our environment. They help to keep the balance of nature in ocean life.

▲ *Sharks play an important role in balancing ocean life.*

▲ *Stingrays are food for sharks.*

For example, sharks eat dangerous fish called stingrays. If there were no sharks, there would be too many stingrays.

Sharks also feed on octopuses. Octopuses eat

▲ *Sharks also eat octopuses.*

lobsters. Without sharks, there would be too many octopuses. Soon there would be no more lobsters in the ocean.

Saving Sharks

There are fewer sharks in the world's oceans today than there used to be. People must begin to protect them.

The first step in saving sharks is to learn more

▲ *Scientists continue to study sharks to learn more about them.*

▲ *Not everyone fears swimming in the water with sharks.*

about them. People need to learn not to fear sharks. They also need to understand the shark's important role in the balance of nature.

Many groups work to teach people about sharks.

▲ *Aquariums help people learn more about sharks.*

Visiting aquariums can also help people learn how sharks live. As people learn more about sharks, they will learn to respect these amazing creatures.

Glossary

canals—tubes or passageways for water

cartilage—soft, flexible tissue in the skeletons of humans and animals

feeding frenzy—the excited eating behavior of a group of sharks

gills—the openings through which a fish breathes

litter—a group of shark pups born at the same time to the same mother

oxygen—a colorless gas in the air. We need oxygen to breathe.

plankton—tiny plants and animals that live in a body of water

predators—creatures that hunt and kill their food

prey—an animal hunted by another animal for food

pups—baby sharks

schools—groups of fish swimming together

Did You Know?

- A person has a better chance of being killed by a bolt of lightning than by a shark.

- The word *shark* likely comes from the German word *schurke* for "villain."

- Some sharks may shed 30,000 teeth in a lifetime.

- Whale sharks are the biggest fish in the sea.

At a Glance

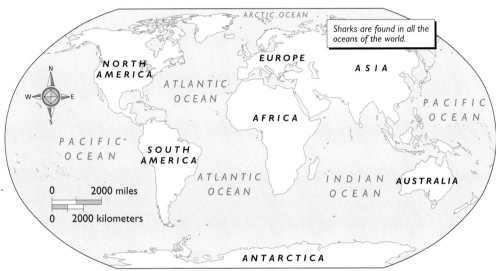

Sharks are found in all the oceans of the world.

Range: Sharks live in warm and cold waters throughout the world. Some live in saltwater. Others live in freshwater.

Size: The smallest shark is the dwarf lantern shark. It is about 5 inches (13 centimeters) long. The largest shark is the whale shark. It can be as long as 60 feet (18 meters) and weigh up to 20 tons.

Species: There are more than 370 different kinds of sharks.

Diet: Sharks eat crabs, fish, sea lions, turtles, sea birds, and even other sharks.

Young: Most sharks give birth to live babies called pups. From two to twenty pups may be born to the mother at one time.

Want to Know More?

At the Library

Brennan, Joseph K. *The Great White Shark*. New York: Workman, 1996.

Fowler, Allan. *The Best Way to See a Shark*. Chicago: Children's Press, 1995.

Holmes, Kevin J. *Sharks*. Mankato, Minn.: Bridgestone Books, 1998.

Markle, Sandra. *Outside and Inside Sharks*. New York: Atheneum, 1996.

On the Web

Mote Marine Laboratory

http://www.marinelab.sarasota.fl.us/

For lots of information about sharks

Shark Surfari

http://www.nationalgeographic.com/features/97/sharks/

For an online quiz about sharks and information from the National Geographic Society

Through the Mail

Shark Research Institute

P.O. Box 40

Princeton, NJ 08540

To get information about the protection of sharks

On the Road

Monterey Bay Aquarium

886 Cannery Row

Monterey, CA 93940-1085

831/648-4800

To visit tropical sharks, touch real sharkskin, and see real shark's teeth

Index

About the Author

Lucia Raatma received her bachelor's degree in English literature from the University of South Carolina and her master's degree in cinema studies from New York University.

She has written a wide range of books for young people. When she is not researching or writing, she enjoys going to movies, playing tennis, and spending time with her husband, daughter, and golden retriever.